A Nap

Written by Caroline Green

Illustrated by Tamara Joubert

Collins

tap

2

tin

...

tap

tin

pan

sit

pan

sit

pat
. . .

nap

pat

nap

🐾 Review: After reading 🐾

Use your assessment from hearing the children read to choose any GPCs or words that need additional practice.

Read 1: Decoding

- Turn to page 6 and ask children to read the word **pan**, sounding out and blending each letter sound. Now turn to page 11 and ask them to do the same with the word **nap**. Ask if they hear the same sounds in the two words.
- Look at the "I spy sounds" pages (14–15). Point to the tongs on the table. Say: These are tongs – "tongs" starts with the /t/ sound. Encourage the children to point to and name other objects beginning with "t". (e.g. *timer, tissues, teacups, teapot, tray, tomatoes, tin opener, tins, tap, tea towel, toaster, table*)
- As they point to and name other objects, ask them to listen for "t" in the middle or end. (e.g. *kettle, list photo/picture*)

Read 2: Vocabulary

- Go back through the book and discuss the pictures. Encourage children to talk about details that stand out for them. Use a dialogic talk model to expand on their ideas and recast them in full sentences as naturally as possible.
- Work together to expand vocabulary by naming objects in the pictures that children do not know.
- Point to the tap, tin and pan on pages 2, 3 and 6. Ask the children to point to the corresponding word. Ask about the object, for example: Why do you think the tap is on? (e.g. *to wash up*)

Read 3: Comprehension

- Encourage the children to choose one of the characters and talk about what they are doing in each of the pictures.
- Ask: How is the family in this book similar to your family? How is it different?
- Turn to pages 14–15 and ask the children to tell you about the kitchen. Ask: What do you have in your kitchen at home that you can also see here? What do you have that is different?